How To

M000119360

"There Are Two Methods That You Can Use To Fill This Memory Book, You Can Choose Whatever Is Convenient For You."

1:

YOU AND YOUR PARTNER WILL BE IN A ROMANTIC SETTING, AND THEN START FILLING THE PAGES ONE BY ONE WITH A LOT OF FUN.

YOU CAN PLAY ROCK PAPER SCISSORS TO SEE WHO WILL BE THE FIRST ONE WHO STARTS ;)

2:

YOU WILL BE THE FIRST ONE WHO START FILLING THE PAGES. AFTER FINISHING LEAVE THE JOURNAL SOMEWHERE FOR YOUR SWEETIE TO FIND. NOW, IT IS THEIR TURN TO DO THE SAME!

This Journal Belongs To

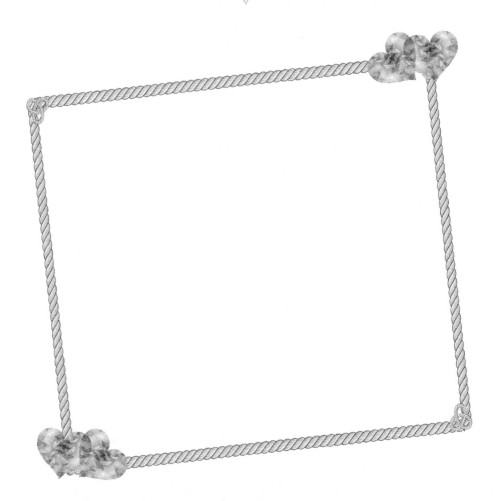

We've Been Together For

Me

When And Where I First Met You

_____

This Is How I Still Remember
Our First Meeting

_____

_____

_____

_____

_____

_____

You

When And Where I First Met You

This Is How I Still Remember Our First Meeting

Me

The First Time You Looked At Me

_____

_____

_____

You

The First Time You Looked At Me

_____

_____

_____

Me

The First Thing You Said To Me

You

The First Thing You Said To Me

_____

_____

_____

Me

My First Impression Of You

_____

_____

_____

You

My First Impression Of You

_____

_____

_____

Me

The First Thing I Liked About You

_____

_____

_____

 You

The First Thing I Liked About You

_____

_____

_____

Me

The First Thing That Attracted Me To You

_____

_____

_____

The First Thing That Attracted Me To You

_____

_____

_____

Me

Our First Date

You

Our First Date

_____

_____

_____

Me

The First Time I Walked By Your Side

_____

_____

_____

You

The First Time I Walked By Your Side

_____

_____

_____

Me

The First Time I Hugged You

_____

_____

_____

The First Time I Hugged You

_____

_____

_____

Me

When And Where I First Kissed You

_____

_____

_____

When And Where I First Kissed You

_____

_____

_____

Me

That First Kiss Made Me

_____

_____

_____

You

That First Kiss Made Me

_____

_____

_____

Me

The First Movie We Watched Together

_____

_____

_____

You

The First Movie We Watched Together

_____

_____

_____

Me

The First Time We Danced Together

_____

_____

_____

You

The First Time We Danced Together

_____

_____

_____

Me

The First Time I Told You I Love You

_____

_____

_____

You

The First Time I Told You I Love You

_____

_____

_____

Me

The First Time We Had Sex Together

_____

_____

_____

You

The First Time We Had Sex Together

Me

The First Time You Cooked For Me

_____

_____

_____

You

The First Time You Cooked For Me

_____

_____

_____

Me

The First Lie I Told You

_____

_____

_____

The First Lie I Told You

_____

_____

_____

Me

My First Birthday With You

_____

_____

_____

You

My First Birthday With You

_____

_____

_____

Me

Our First Fight

_____

_____

_____

You

Our First Fight

Me

Our First Vacation

You

Our First Vacation

_____

_____

_____

Me

Our First Christmas Together

_____

_____

_____

You

Our First Christmas Together

_____

_____

_____

Me

Our First Valentine's Day Together

_____

_____

_____

You

Our First Valentine's Day Together

_____

_____

_____

Me

Our First Sunset Watching

_____

_____

_____

You

Our First Sunset Watching

_____

_____

_____

Me

*Our First Photo Together
That Was Taken By Me*

_____

_____

_____

You

Our First Photo Together That Was Taken By Me

_____

_____

_____

Me

Our Best Romantic Moment

_____

_____

_____

You

Our Best Romantic Moment

_____

_____

_____

The Funniest Memory I Had With You

_____

_____

_____

You

The Funniest Memory I Had With You

_____

_____

_____

Me

The Best Compliment You Said That Was Meaningful To Me

You

The Best Compliment You Said That Was Meaningful To Me

_____

_____

_____

Me

This Is How I Learned And I Got Over
That Disappointing Time In Our Relationship

_____

_____

_____

You

This Is How I Learned And I Got Over
That Disappointing Time In Our Relationship

_____

_____

_____

Me

A Place Where We've Had A Great Time Together

_____

_____

_____

You

A Place Where We've Had A Great Time Together

_____

_____

_____

Me

I Still Remember That Rainy Day

_____

_____

_____

You

I Still Remember That Rainy Day

_____

_____

_____

Me

The Most Memorable Gift I've Got From You

_____

_____

_____

You

The Most Memorable Gift I've Got From You

_____

_____

_____

Me

That Time When You Took Care Of Me

_____

_____

_____

You

That Time When You Took Care Of Me

_____

_____

_____

Me

The Most Amazing Thing We've Done Together

_____

_____

_____

You

The Most Amazing Thing We've Done Together

_____

_____

_____

Me

The Cheapest And Simplest Fun We've Had

_____

_____

_____

You

The Cheapest And Simplest Fun We've Had

_____

_____

_____

Me

Things You Did That Made Me Smile

_____

_____

_____

You

Things You Did That Made Me Smile

_____

_____

_____

Me

The Most Memorable Miracle
We Experienced Together

_____

_____

_____

You

The Most Memorable Miracle We Experienced Together

_____

_____

_____

Me

This Is What I Missed Most About You When You Were Apart

_____

_____

_____

You

This Is What I Missed Most About You When You Were Apart

_____

_____

_____

Me

That Time When You Helped Me

_____

_____

_____

You

That Time When You Helped Me

_____

_____

_____

I Can't Forget This Text You Sent Me

_____

_____

_____

You

I Can't Forget This Text You Sent Me

_____

_____

_____

Me

A Book I Remember Reading With You

_____

_____

_____

You

A Book I Remember Reading With You

_____

_____

_____

Me

The Best Advice I've Got From You

_____

_____

_____

You

The Best Advice I've Got From You

_____

_____

_____

Me

A Secret About Me That Only You Know

_____

_____

_____

You

A Secret About Me That Only You Know

_____

_____

_____

Me

A Special Dream I Shared With You

_____

_____

_____

You

A Special Dream I Shared With You

_____

_____

_____

Me

The Most Romantic Letter
I Received From You

_____

_____

_____

You

The Most Romantic Letter
I Received From You

_____

_____

_____

Me

This Is How You Made Me A Better Person

_____

_____

_____

You

This Is How You Made Me A Better Person

_____

_____

_____

Me

The Promise I Made To You

_____

_____

_____

You

The Promise I Made To You

_____

_____

_____

Me

A Special Nickname I Got From You

_____

_____

_____

You

A Special Nickname I Got From You

_____

_____

_____

Me

A Time We've Laughed The Hardest

_____

_____

_____

You

A Time We've Laughed The Hardest

_____

_____

_____

Me

The Best Trip We Took Together

_____

_____

_____

You

The Best Trip We Took Together

_____

_____

_____

Me

The Biggest Adventure We've Had

_____
_____
_____

You

The Biggest Adventure We've Had

_____

_____

_____

The Funniest Joke You Told Me

_____

_____

_____

You

The Funniest Joke You Told Me

_____

_____

_____

Me

Something You Did That Made Me Feel Loved & Cared

_____

_____

_____

You

Something You Did That Made Me Feel Loved & Cared

_____

_____

_____

Me

_____

_____

_____

_____

_____

_____

_____

You

_____

_____

_____

_____

_____

_____

_____

_____

Made in the USA
Monee, IL
21 August 2021

76219698R00066